THE BATTLE OF BLENHEIM

August 13, 1704

The When and Why Books

The aim of this series is to take a familiar event in history and examine the cause and effect so that it no longer stands isolated from its background. Each book is clearly written for the ten to fourteen year olds and is fully illustrated with line drawings, many in two colours.

THE
BATTLE OF BLENHEIM

AUGUST 13, 1704

JOHN HENRY CROCKATT

Illustrations by
Graham Humphreys

LUTTERWORTH PRESS

GUILDFORD AND LONDON

First published 1973

ISBN o 7188 1914 4

COPYRIGHT © 1973 BY JOHN HENRY CROCKATT

PRINTED IN GREAT BRITAIN
BY EBENEZER BAYLIS AND SON LTD
THE TRINITY PRESS, WORCESTER, AND LONDON

CONTENTS

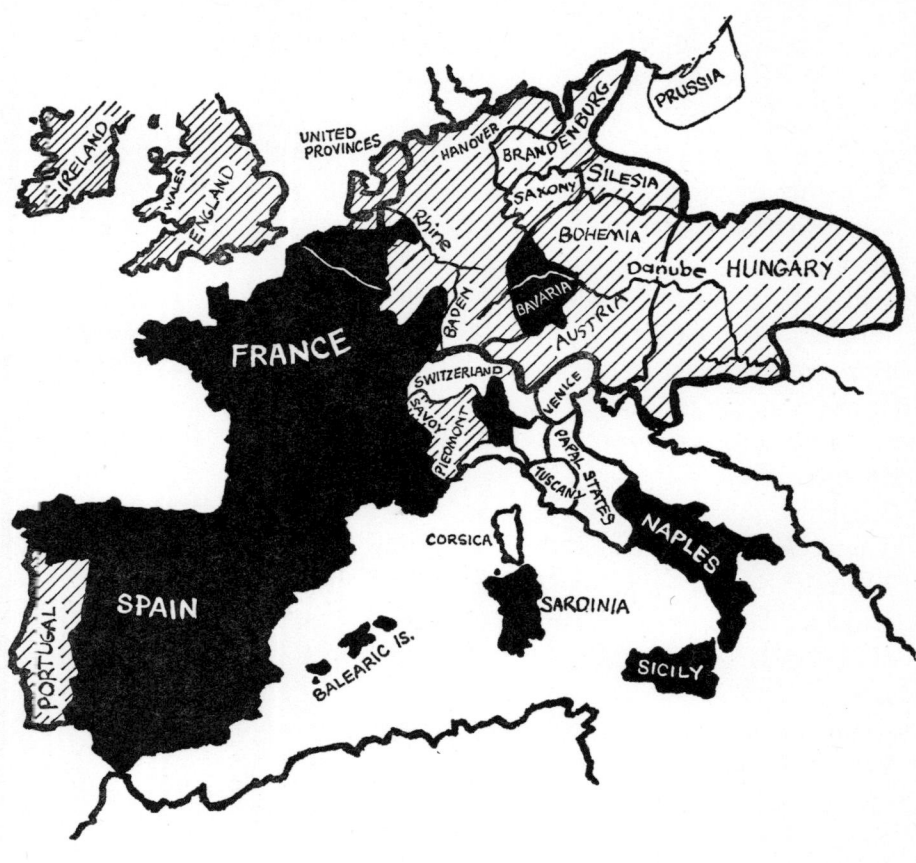

BRITAIN AND ALLIES   **FRANCE AND ALLIES**

The map shows the division of Europe during the War of the Spanish Succession

ENGLAND AND EUROPE

EARLY in 1702 King William III was riding near Hampton Court when his horse stumbled over a mole-hill and fell, with the result that the king broke his collar bone, and, never a strong man, within days, succumbed to pleurisy and died. He had ruled England for fourteen years and Holland for much longer and both kingdoms had witnessed his life-long absorption in the task of preventing Louis XIV from devouring Europe in the name of France and the Catholic religion.

Time and again in the second half of the 17th century William, first as Prince of Orange and subsequently as King of England, had stood defiant and checked the ambitions of Louis XIV, the 'Sun King' of France, who had built for himself one of the most splendid Courts ever known in Europe. Having saved the Dutch Republic William became King of England and spent the rest of his life labouring to upset Louis' plans.

Not long before, when William was a small boy, the little Dutch Republic had fought first Oliver Cromwell's admirals and later those of King Charles II to decide to which nation should go the command of the North Sea and the Channel. These Anglo-Dutch wars, purely naval in character, arose out of the commercial rivalry existing between the two countries. Both the Dutch and English were forward looking peoples, who enjoyed greater freedom than the subjects of the Sun

King of France. While, in Admiral Blake's time, the English seemed to have the advantage of the Dutch, after Cromwell's death affairs took a turn for the worse. Charles II was not long on the throne before the Dutch fleet in 1667 sailed up the Medway, bombarded the naval town of Chatham, and then retired to Holland with the King's flagship in tow.

Louis XIV of France

The Glorious Revolution of 1688 was a landmark in English history. William and his wife, Mary, were presented with the Crown on condition that they agreed to safeguard the constitutional rights of Parliament. Dutch William had been only too pleased to accept an invitation from the great men in the land of both political parties, Whig and Tory, to make a landing in the West Country and oust the Catholic King James II. But it was not through love of England that the Dutchman had finally decided to make his bid. He needed more soldiers with which to maintain the struggle against Louis XIV and England would prove a useful source of recruitment.

With the Crown sitting comfortably on William's head, England and Holland patched up their commercial differences, and, in face of Catholic Louis' threat to the Protestant cause, remained firm allies for years to come.

At Charles II's death in 1685 England was back where she was in early Stuart times, a second rate power with no army worthy of the name. James II's three disastrous years on the throne hardly improved matters and by the time the little Dutchman made his landing in the West Country the country's standing had reached a very low water mark.

But in William III, the English, unknown to themselves, were fortunate. Badly in need of soldiers to join his sturdy Dutchmen in the Protestant crusade, William pushed forward recruitment and the ranks multiplied till he was able to build a sizeable and well-trained force capable of playing an honourable part on continental battlefields. As a general, William, who lost more battles than he won, can hardly be rated a success, but as a statesman he was outstanding.

The problem facing Europe in the months before William's death was one which, if not faced up to properly, could bring William's life work crashing about his feet. On the morning of November 9, 1700, King Louis XIV of France received the news that Europe had awaited for years. Charles II, King of Spain, was dead and the Spanish Hapsburg line was ended. For forty years this poor invalid, as weak in body as in mind, had time and again ruined the predictions of European statesmen by hanging on to life by a thin thread right into middle age. Nor did he finally give up the struggle without first making a will, leaving Spain and her widespread possessions in the Netherlands and Italy, not to speak of the New

World and elsewhere, to his great-nephew, Philip, the Duke of Anjou, and his successors.

So rather than permit the dismemberment of his vast empire, the dying Charles, with the Pope's blessing, made it all over to the man who was also the grandson of the French King, a young man whom he felt could be relied upon to maintain it intact, if necessary with the help of French bayonets. But would the King of France be prepared to repudiate agreements previously reached with

Philip of Anjou, King of Spain

William III to partition the inheritance? In short, would Louis dare to run the risk of war? Never in all his fifty-seven years on the throne had Louis been faced with such a decision. But, realizing that refusal to accept the Spanish king's wishes would hand the entire inheritance to the Austrian Archduke Charles, son of Leopold, the Holy Roman Emperor, Louis soon made up his mind.

On that fateful Tuesday, November 16, 1700, the ageing Louis, with his nineteen-year-old grandson at his side, confronted his courtiers. "Gentlemen," he announced, "here is the King of Spain." At this, the Spanish ambassador fell on his knees and exclaimed, as he kissed the hand of his new Sovereign, "The Pyrenees have ceased to exist".

One after another the crowned heads of Europe recognized Philip as the lawful King of Spain and when at last he entered Madrid the Spanish people took him to their hearts. At this blatant threat to the balance of power, which Dutch William had fought all his life to preserve, Holland would have liked to take up arms once again, but the English Parliament would have none of it and William III had grudgingly to accept the situation, well aware that little Holland, for all her gallantry, could not withstand Louis single-handed.

Only the Emperor of Austria, who had hoped to grab a good part of the Spanish possessions for his son, the Archduke Charles, took action. Infuriated that the Sun King should have flouted earlier agreements to partition the Spanish Empire on Charles II's death, he immediately sent Austrian troops under Prince Eugene of Savoy into the Spanish possessions of Northern Italy, which provoked Louis to dispatch a considerable French force for their defence.

Not just content to accept the will, Louis next, without warning, seized a line of fortresses in Belgium, garrisoned under treaty rights by Dutch troops and constituting the main barrier of the Netherlands against French invasion. Beneath the dynastic antagonism, which Louis' high-handed action had provoked, lay a deadly commercial rivalry. The English were fearful at the prospect of France obtaining not only special trading concessions in Spanish America, but control of Spanish Mediterranean ports. In short, the thought of a strong Spain, however indirectly united to a France grown fat on the riches of Spanish America, was as alarming to England as the seizure of the barrier towns was to the Dutch.

On September 7, 1701, England and Holland, the two great seafaring countries, formed a Grand Alliance with the Emperor of Austria for the purpose of restoring the balance of power in Europe. But, as yet, there was no declaration of war, not at least until Louis showed that there was no end to his arrogance with his recognition of the right of James Stuart, the Old Pretender, to inherit the English throne after the death in September, 1701, of James II, his father. To a people who in 1689 had deliberately exchanged Protestant William for the obstinate Catholic James, this was the crowning insult, which even the complacent English were not prepared to tolerate. It was also the biggest mistake of Louis' career, and a flagrant breach of previous agreements.

But it was precisely at this moment that the Dutch King of England chose to die. William, a hero to his native Dutchmen, had deserved better of his English subjects, who never liked him. Yet, for all his boorish ways and partiality for his Dutch cronies who received all the best jobs, he did much for England by his policy of building up her armed forces. It was William too who first envisaged the importance of gaining mastery in the Mediterranean. In fact, whatever his tactical shortcomings on the field of battle, his strategic thinking, which Marlborough, the English military commander, was to build upon with such flair, was most sound. "There was a time," said William towards the end of his life, "when I should have been glad to have been delivered out of my troubles, but I own I see another

James II, who lost his throne to William and Mary

scene and could wish to live a little longer."

Marlborough's scene it proved to be, for it was William who, at the end of his life, entrusted to him the nation's safety. The fragile little king with the heart of a lion had for years realized that without England's support Holland stood small chance of fending off Louis' overwhelming forces. Alas, by only a few short months, he did not live to see an Anglo-Dutch army under a superb English commander challenge the might of France.

William was fifty-two when he died exhausted by all his efforts in the Protestant cause. Marlborough, at the same age, took over the burden, and, as a result, gave his country ten years of unbroken victory and raised her to heights never before dreamt of.

On May 18, 1702, therefore, war was declared by England, Holland and Austria and the war of the Spanish Succession was let loose upon Europe. The arrogant king of France must be held chiefly responsible, though he little knew what surprises lay in store for him at the hands of John Churchill, soon to be created Duke of Marlborough.

King William III, Prince of Orange

During the second half of the 17th century Louis had fought a number of wars, notably against the English and the Dutch, but at the start of the new century he found himself taking on more enemies than ever before. Besides England, Holland and the Austrian Empire the Alliance included Denmark and almost the whole of Germany, of which Prussia and Hanover formed a substantial part. By the time Blenheim was fought, the Alliance was swelled by the inclusion both of Portugal and the little kingdom of Savoy lying at the western extremity of Italy.

The war of the Spanish Succession was no different from other wars of those days in that it was fought with close relatives in opposing camps. Queen Anne, who succeeded William III, found herself opposed to her half-brother James, the Old Pretender, son of James II, while the Sun King himself was her cousin. The Duke of Berwick, a fine soldier who had much success against the Allies in Spain, fought against his uncle, Marlborough, notably at the seige of Lille in 1709, while Marlborough's celebrated partner, Prince Eugene, who fought in the Emperor's service, was opposed at Oudenarde by his first cousin, Marshal Vendôme.

To begin with, against Louis' 200,000 men, the Allies fielded a quarter of a million soldiers, of which England's initial contribution was a mere 50,000. As for ships, Louis could boast only eighty, hardly enough for him to defend the world-wide Spanish Empire and the shores of France. Furthermore, as the war progressed Louis, as we have seen, lost to the Allies both Portugal and Savoy, though the German Kingdom of Bavaria, whose late Prince had, under

Queen Mary, joint sovereign with William

the First Partition Treaty, been offered the Spanish Crown, remained to the end loyal to Catholic France. Finally, to find France and Spain close allies, after nearly 300 years of rivalry, was an extraordinary turn of events.

JOHN CHURCHILL

John Churchill was born in 1650, the eldest son of Sir Winston Churchill, a Dorset squire, who had fought for King Charles I in the Civil War and in consequence lost his estates. As a boy, John attended St. Paul's School in London, but learning had little appeal and at the age of fourteen John became a page at the Court of King Charles II.

John was soon chosen to join the household of James, Duke of York, the King's brother, who, in 1667, saw to it that the handsome young man with the charming manner, received a commission in the First Foot Guards (renamed, after Waterloo, the Grenadiers), in which capacity he was posted to Tangiers where he received his baptism of fire fighting the Moors. No sooner had John returned to England, having earned a considerable military reputation, than he was sent abroad again, but this time only across the Channel.

In Flanders John served under James, Duke of Monmouth, the King's natural son, and a favourite of the Whigs; then, after gaining experience of continental warfare, he returned to Court, a Colonel now, with tales of Turenne and other Marshals of France.

With his character now matured by experience, the young Churchill was much sought after by the women who swarmed around the Court of a King well-named "The Merry Monarch". Charles, for all his faults, at least sought to encourage laughter

Sarah Churchill, later the Duchess of Marlborough

and entertainment, which he felt his subjects deserved after the long, bleak years of Cromwell's austerity. Churchill too liked the fairer sex, so he was constantly dancing attendance on the Court beauties, even one or two closely connected with the King. But this more frivolous side of his nature underwent a change when he fell in love with and married Sarah Jennings.

She was fifteen and he twenty-six and they were far from rich, besides which their temperaments were entirely opposite. Sarah, the vivacious Court beauty, was sharp-tongued, outspoken and frequently downright rude. The Colonel was calm,

courteous and a model of patience. But, for all their differences in temperament, the young couple were deeply in love and remained so for the rest of their lives. But it took a patient man to withstand some of Sarah's sallies. Her behaviour could at times be outrageous and she could easily resort to gutter language and violence.

However, as well as bringing John great happiness the

The Battle of Sedgemoor in 1685 brought victory for King James's men

union was to advance his career. Sarah was an attendant upon the Princess Anne, the plump and plain second daughter of James, Duke of York, with whom she formed an intimate friendship, which, so long as it lasted, maintained Churchill's great position. When, years later, Duchess Sarah's overbearing attitude towards Queen Anne brought an end to the friendship, Churchill's power crumbled and he and Sarah went into exile. But in these early days, and indeed for years to come, Princess Anne and Sarah Churchill met almost daily and, when apart, wrote to each other, signing their letters with pet names of their own invention. The Princess was "Mrs. Morley" and Sarah "Mrs. Freeman", while Churchill, much to his embarrassment, found himself referred to in this intimate circle as "Mr. Freeman".

At Charles II's death in 1685, Churchill, now a Major-General, continued to serve James II, the new King. Unfortunately, James had neither his brother's charm, wit nor ability. He proved therefore neither popular nor successful; for, quite the contrary, he was stubborn, stupid and cruel. No sooner was the crown on his head than the young Duke of Monmouth, whose life the young Churchill had saved at the Siege of Maastricht, slipped away from Holland and landed in the West Country to claim the Crown on behalf of the Protestant cause. But he struck too soon, for James had not yet had time to inflict 'Popery' on his subjects, the majority of whom, for the time being at least, quietly accepted him.

Monmouth's hope of support from the gentry proved a disappointment. They simply kept away and all that Monmouth was able to assemble were a few thousand simple-minded countrymen with a hatred of Catholics. But there was no turning back. King James meantime dispatched westwards General Churchill whose appearance before Bridport coincided with the appointment of the Earl of Faversham, a fat and lazy Frenchman of no military experience, as Churchill's military superior.

The evening of July 4, 1685, saw the Royal Army encamped behind a deep ditch at Sedgemoor. It was a misty, moonless night when Faversham ponderously removed his boots and settled down to sleep. Not so his second-in-command. He remained wide awake, seeing to the royal army's defences, which was just as well as the rebels were picking their way stealthily across Sedgemoor, bent on a surprise attack. At length Monmouth's ramshackle force, many equipped with no more than bill-hooks and scythes, stumbled across the ditch. A pistol went off and Lord Churchill's men were alerted. His slumbers disturbed, Faversham pulled on his boots and before the mirror, adjusted his cravat. But Churchill, without fuss, had the situation well under control and the resultant battle, such as it was, lasted only a short while.

Within the hour the roar of musketry ceased and the "Protestant Hero" disappeared in the mist, only to be caught later and hauled before his unforgiving uncle, James II, as a preliminary to an unpleasant end on Tower Hill. Faversham's ineptitude had allowed John Churchill to win the last battle ever fought on English soil, though it was Faversham, not Churchill, whom a grateful sovereign honoured with the much coveted Order of the Garter.

Judge Jeffrey's "Bloody Assize", which followed hard on the battle, disgusted Churchill as much as it did most Englishmen. The bloodthirsty revenge which James II took on the rebels was abominably cruel as well as fatal to the King's popularity. "That marble", Lord Churchill once remarked, "is as incapable of feeling compassion as the King's heart."

Churchill's able conduct at Sedgemoor was proof of his loyalty to the Sovereign. It took the next three years to convince him that James, through his Catholic policy, was out of sympathy with the English people. In addition to being a thorough royalist Churchill, above all, was a stout supporter of the Church of England, with an Englishman's dislike of foreign ideas, which the Catholic religion of King James personified. The mighty Louis of France was, after all, its champion and he was hardly popular in England.

When, at the end of 1688, Dutch William landed in the small South Devon port of Torbay, Churchill remained loyal until almost everyone had deserted James, and, then, secretly, he stole away one night from his Catholic master's camp to offer William his sword. Churchill's conduct is hard to excuse. His eye was clearly on the main chance, however great his protestations that "he saw our religion and country were in danger of being destroyed". Churchill's reputation for duplicity, moreover, grew justifiably out of the secretive manner of his desertion rather than the desertion itself. Well might the unfortunate James cry out "God help me! Even my children have deserted me". James's own daughter, Anne, encouraged by those very same Churchills, ran out on him at the last minute.

William was already a European figure when he became, at the beginning of 1689, joint sovereign alongside his wife Mary, the staunchly Protestant daughter of the recently deposed James. One of William's first acts was to confer on Churchill the Earldom of Marlborough and send him to Flanders and later to Ireland, where he enhanced his military reputation.

Then, quite suddenly, Churchill was dismissed because he openly criticized the King for giving all the best and most lucrative jobs to Dutchmen. For several years he remained unemployed. For all his exceptional gifts, William could never fully trust him and for a short time even had him locked up in the Tower of London on a charge of treason, which was soon proved groundless.

It was only when the King's health began to deteriorate towards the turn of the century that the fortunes of the Marlboroughs began to improve. In 1698 John had all his offices restored to him by a king who, for all his distrust of the man, was well aware of the Earl's exceptional talents. Just before his death William appointed Marlborough to a high diplomatic post combined with the supreme command of all the English soldiers abroad.

THE CAMPAIGNS OF 1702–1703

ANNE had only been on the throne a few weeks before
Parliament, in concert with the Dutch States-General, and
the Holy Roman Emperor, declared war against France and
Spain. At the time, Marlborough, as special ambassador at the
Dutch capital and Captain-General of the English forces in the
Netherlands, had entire direction of Allied war strategy. This
basically had two aims :- the reconquest of the Netherlands and
the wresting from France of control of the Mediterranean. At
the outbreak of war King Louis' men-o-war sailed the Atlantic
and Mediterranean with impunity. Besides, a good part of
Italy was in French hands and most Mediterranean islands
were occupied by French and Spanish soldiers. But it took
only a year or two for the Allies to bring about a complete
transformation.

The war of the Spanish Succession was one of the first
major European Wars, with four quite distinct areas of
operation. First and foremost was the fighting around Belgium
and its borders, in which Marlborough himself, as a field
commander, played so dominant a role. There was constant
fighting also around West Germany and the Rhine as well as in
the hills of Northern Italy, if only for a while, and to the south-
west in Spain, the country whose destiny had given rise to the
conflict.

Naval operations began with Sir George Rooke's unsuccessful attempt to capture the Spanish Atlantic port of Cadiz. Shortly afterwards, however, in 1703, he sank a great number of enemy ships and took home quantities of bullion captured from the Spanish. Weeks before the battle of Blenheim was fought the great rock of Gibraltar fell to the English, who remained in possession for the rest of the war despite enemy attempts to regain it. A month later Rooke decisively defeated the French fleet off Malaga, further east along the coast from Gibraltar.

Although Marlborough was in overall charge of Allied strategy, including the naval aspects, he was no free agent, as were Napoleon, Frederick the Great or, for that matter, Louis XIV himself. Like everyone else Marlborough was a subject of Queen Anne and answerable to an ever watchful Parliament for his actions. With so many politicians actively opposed to his Mediterranean and Continental policy Marlborough, a man of iron nerve and high moral courage, though given to fits of depression, had to make but one mistake to bring about his own downfall. Napoleon and other great Captains, on the other hand, could miscalculate, as they some-times did, and lose their battles without being called to account by their Governments.

One special comfort to Marlborough, as he left annually on campaign, was the presence in Whitehall of Sydney Godolphin, the General's close friend and loyal colleague, who, like Marlborough, had in youth been reared at the Merry Monarch's mischievous Court. By family tradition, a West Country Tory, Godolphin, was essentially a royalist,

Sydney Godolphin,
Lord of the Treasury

unfettered by Party. While Marlborough framed the Grand strategy and fought the battles, Lord Treasurer Godolphin—"Mr. Montgomery" to Queen Anne—looked after the purse-strings at home. In Sydney Godolphin, Marlborough possessed a true friend in whom he could at all times confide, as witness the voluminous correspondence exchanged between the two while Marlborough was away on campaign. In sharing the conduct of the great war they were in reality joint prime ministers, their friendship being further strengthened by the marriage of the Lord Treasurer's son to the Captain-General's daughter.

With a European war on his hands Marlborough, virtually Prime Minister, Foreign Secretary and Commander-in-Chief rolled into one, certainly had a formidable task ahead of him.

26

Louis' soldiers had, like Cromwell's Ironsides before them, gained a reputation for invincibility. Although William III had succeeded in frustrating Louis' invasion plans against Holland, it was quite another matter to inflict defeat on the French army. The well-drilled soldiers of the Sun King needed no convincing of their superiority. Nevertheless the French high command was much more pre-occupied with siege warfare than fighting battles. For years continental warfare resembled a game of chess, with its endless manœuvring, enlivened, only occasionally, by a pitched battle.

But now, with the imaginative Marlborough and the great Prince Eugene of Savoy assembling their battalions, the old rules were about to be violently overthrown, for Marlborough believed, no less than the Prince, that manœuvre should have but one end in view, to bring the enemy to battle—and at a disadvantage. The war, the Allied leadership was convinced, could only be won and France humbled by a decision on the battlefield. Anticipating the Germans of a later age, the Duke also believed in swift movement, of which he gave sublime examples not only before Blenheim, but in the opening stages of the battle of Oudenarde and, above all, at the very end of his unmatched career when he completely outmanœuvred Marshal Villars by a series of rapid marches culminating in the capture of Bouchain. The French on that occasion were left abashed at such a finale.

At the same time, it would be wrong to infer that Marlborough shunned siege warfare. On the contrary, he took every fortress to which he laid siege. In fact, he took more

The War of the Spanish Succession started with a number of Engl

aval victories, including the one which led to the capture of Gibraltar

fortresses than any other English general. But, as far as he was concerned, siege warfare was purely a means to an end, and by no means an end in itself. In the final analysis Marlborough sought victory, devastating and complete, on the field of battle, where his many and varied talents received their greatest scope. Indeed, but for the exaggerated caution of his Dutch allies, he might well have achieved even more. He frequently drove the French into such an exposed position that he had them at his mercy, but the Dutch, terrified of putting all to the test, despite the odds in their favour, simply refused to advance.

What the Dutch deplored in Marlborough was his gambler's streak, an idiosyncrasy of all great Captains, from Julius Caesar to Napoleon. With allies as unco-operative and defensive-minded as the Dutch, Marlborough had constant need of his enormous reserves of patience. A less courteous and tactful general might have split the Alliance, but Marlborough, the diplomat supreme, as well as the master of war, kept his temper, whatever toll it took of his health and whatever the headaches he suffered as a result. Marlborough's great schemes for the destruction of the French in Italy, Spain, the South of France and on the high seas, were a closed book to these stolid Dutchmen who saw nothing beyond the defence of their own borders.

Marlborough's campaigns followed a familiar pattern. They began in early Spring and were concluded in time for Christmas. In his continual quest for victory the Duke extended the campaigning season beyond the traditional span. In the very depth of winter, however, conditions were quite unsuitable for waging war. Roads became mud-tracks, hours of daylight were restricted and there was not enough hay to feed the horses. Under these circumstances, the Duke had no option but to strike camp and either go home to grapple with the grasping politicians at Westminster or ride in his coach the length and breadth of Europe in order to keep the Grand Alliance in good repair.

Only a small proportion of Marlborough's soldiers were English, the majority hailing from many different kingdoms, duchies and principalities. Holland, Denmark, Belgium and Prussia probably supplied the bulk, apart from the Austrians led by Prince Eugene, who made a notable contribution. There was a limit to the number of English soldiers that Marlborough could muster in the Low Countries as so many had to be shipped further afield to fit into his great strategic plans. They were needed, for instance, to help our Portuguese allies fight the Spaniards, they were needed in the West Indies. Some were also sent on various combined operations off the Mediterranean and Atlantic coasts.

The foot soldiers' weapon in battle at this time was the musket, deadly accurate to within a hundred yards, but, beyond that distance, unreliable. Much of Marlborough's success was due to his splendid infantry, never more than a third of which was English. It was trained by Marlborough, during the winter lull, to move in four-line formations against the French six or eight, with extended wings to outflank the enemy. Infantry tactics had undergone a good deal of change with the introduction of the ring bayonet, enabling the

31

musketeer to discard the pike and fire his shot through the ring which clamped the bayonet to the gun, and then stab the enemy with the same weapon.

The cavalry was the Duke's special love and during more than one battle the Commander-in-Chief could be spotted, sword in hand, galloping full tilt against the enemy, revelling in the sheer danger and excitement of close combat. This habit of temporarily shedding the responsibilities of general-ship for those of a junior cornet nearly cost him his life at the battle of Ramillies in 1706.

In the 18th century cavalry was used to best advantage in open country, like the Danube plains around Blenheim, but where hedges and ditches and other natural obstacles abounded, its movement was restricted, as at Oudenarde, which was essentially an infantry battle. In Marlborough's time cavalry could either engage the enemy with sword or pistol or some-times even musket. Having discharged their firearms they could continue to fight by sword or ride off into safety—an advantage they had over the infantry, who just had to stick it out. Marlborough, with his complete understanding of their roles, got the very best out of both arms of the service. The artillery, commanded by the famous Colonel Blood, Marlborough kept under his own personal direction, sighting his guns, as at Blenheim, with infinite care, so as to ensure their maximum effectiveness in support of the other arms. Marlborough's guns frequently adopted a mobile role, firing sometimes at point-blank range.

Marlborough fought eleven campaigns in all. The first two

(of 1702 and 1703), which preceded Blenheim, tested his patience to the very limit. Having obtained Holland's reluctant agreement that he should command all the Anglo-Dutch forces and not merely the English contingent, Marlborough lost no time in taking the offensive. He quickly manœuvred the French army into such an awkward position that he had only to attack for them to be annihilated. But the Field Deputies, civilian Dutchmen, attached to the Duke's head-quarters to curb his rashness, would have none of it, and so allowed the first of many an opportunity to slip by. The Dutch, being single-minded in their pre-occupation over the defence of their motherland, were fearful, especially at first, that this foreign general, might, with his yearning for battle, lead them straight to disaster.

So, instead of brilliant victory and an end to the war, Marlborough, a Duke by now, had to content himself with a series of clever strategies and with the reduction of a number of fortresses. By so doing, he had the doubtful satisfaction of at least gaining Dutch confidence, small consolation when these dour burghers so frequently robbed him of his chance of victory. By the finish of his second campaign, towards the end of 1703, Marlborough's patience was really stretched to the limit. "I would much sooner die," he wrote to Godolphin, "than face another campaign under such conditions." But now, with 1704 about to burst upon the world, he had other plans which the course of events dictated.

THE MARCH TO THE DANUBE

IN the latter half of the year 1703 two new problems occurred. A full-scale revolt against imperial Austria had broken out in Hungary, and then, in September, for purely selfish motives, Bavaria entered the war on the side of France. Thus Marlborough clearly saw how dangerous was the threat to the Allied position in Southern Germany where French armies could now safely install themselves in a position to strike at the imperial capital of Vienna. Thus with her neighbours, the Hungarians and the Bavarians, lined up against her, Austria was now exposed to attack from East and West. Only a rescue operation from outside could save her.

The man who first suggested to Marlborough that he should take his army away from Flanders and march it half-way across Europe to the Danube was the charming and cultivated Austrian Ambassador in London, Count Wratislaw. It caused no surprise to the Duke, who no doubt had considered so obvious a plan to save the house of Hapsburg. The difficulty lay in its execution. There were many pitfalls to be overcome. First of all, the Dutch, obsessed by the threat to their own frontiers, were bound to be hostile to such a plan. In the second place, secrecy was vital. Not only the French, but the Dutch, and indeed the English politicians, would have to be kept in the dark. With all the administrative problems involved, a march into the heart of the continent would require

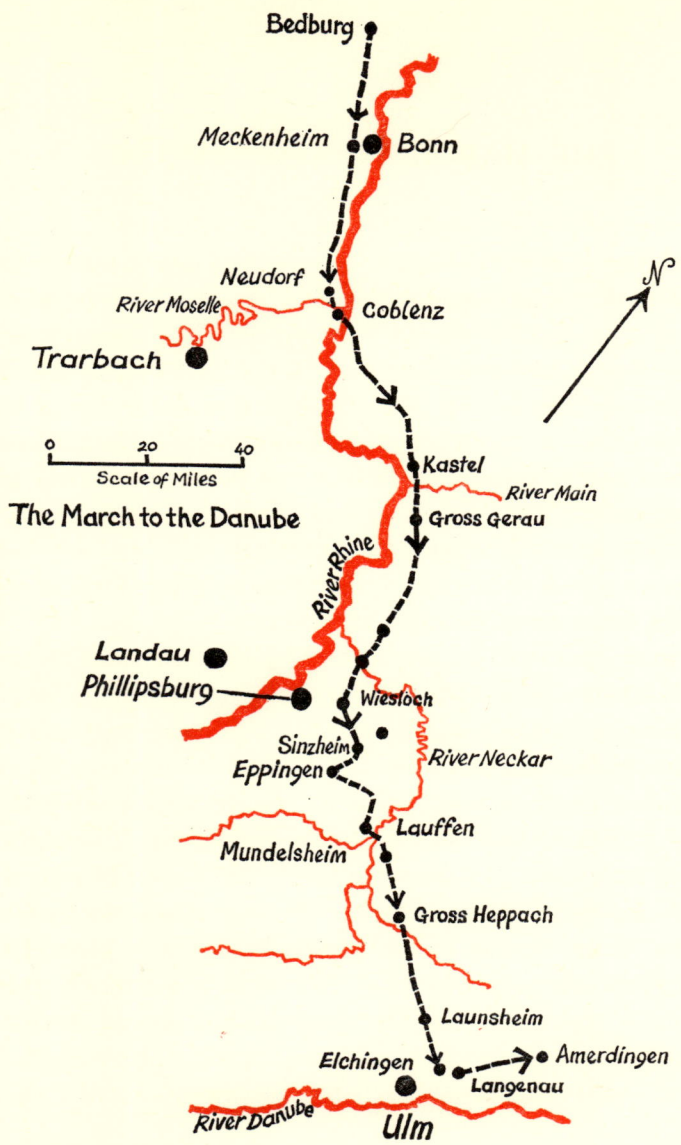

The route taken by Marlborough's troops on the march south

meticulous planning. Food supplies, footwear, fodder for the horses, staging camps, hospital facilities and a host of other essentials would have to be arranged behind closed doors.

Fortunately Marlborough was not only a superb administrator, but also the most secretive of men, and just as well, as he would require all his guile to hoodwink not only the French as to his plans, but the Dutch and indeed the politicians in England also. He warmed from the very first to Wratislaw's suggestion. Top-secret discussions between the Austrian diplomat and the Captain-General continued throughout the winter, but it was not till April 1704 that Marlborough finally agreed to take the gamble.

The Danube plan was easy enough to conceive, but it took a genius to carry it through. It was easy for the Emperor of Austria, through his ambassador in London, to ask Marlborough to come to his rescue. It was quite another matter to accept the invitation and then effect this most difficult assignment. Nevertheless, the Duke assumed single-handed responsibility for conducting his army into Central Europe, with neither Dutch permission nor that of his colleagues at Westminster. It was a decision of high courage, for Marlborough knew the risk he was taking and the certainty that failure would let loose a torrent of anger against him and bring his career to ruins. But once committed, he spared no effort to ensure that the plan would work, as far as humanly possible, without a hitch.

In the event, the Duke's original scheme to invade France from the East by way of the Moselle valley served as a useful

36

Queen Anne, the English queen throughout the War of the Spanish Succession

'blind' to the French and to the world at large. For a troop concentration along the Rhine as far south as Coblenz pointed to the Moselle, yet would serve equally well for an advance on the Danube. In January 1704, only after much hesitation, the Dutch States-General gave its assent to Marlborough's Moselle plan, even to the extent of contributing Dutch troops, but Marlborough was careful to say nothing about going all the way to the Danube. By the time that Marlborough had finally committed himself, only Wratislaw, the Emperor of Austria and the Emperor's loyal servant, the Prince Eugene, recently

37

released from his desk for more important business in the field, were parties to the plan. The Queen and Godolphin knew of certain schemes afoot to save the Empire, but at this stage the Duke, himself a born conspirator, allowed them to know no more. To Sarah he wisely said nothing.

As well as constituting a large scale rescue bid, the march to the Danube enabled Marlborough to escape from his tiresome Dutch colleagues, who had so successfully prevented him from trying to win the war on the battlefields of Northern Europe. A change of scene was needed and something really decisive to prevent the war from stagnating year after year. The fact that the Dutch were eventually persuaded over the Moselle plan did them credit and in the end acted to their advantage. Marlborough's prediction that his departure South would encourage the French to leave the Netherlands and chase after him, actually came about.

The march, as it turned out, was a triumph. "The annals of the British army contain no more heroic episode than this march from the North Sea to the Danube. The strategy which conceived, the secrecy and skill which performed and the superb victory which crowned the enterprise have always ranked among the finest examples of the art of war." So wrote Sir Winston Churchill in his biography of his great ancestor. From first to last the enemy were deceived. Marlborough's army of 40,000, of whom only 10,000 were English, reached Coblenz at the beginning of May 1704. Here, instead of turning up the Moselle valley, as he was expected to do, Marlborough moved east towards the Rhine, where he had boats built as though for an attack on Strasbourg. Meanwhile, far away to the north, the French army had fulfilled the Duke's prediction by pulling out of the Netherlands and heading south-east. But already the French were mystified and Marlborough had no difficulty in concentrating his forces in south-east Germany.

Leaving the Rhine behind him, Marlborough rode ahead with his cavalry straight for Bavaria, closely followed by the

The march to the Danube took the soldiers through some beautiful countryside

infantry, commanded by his younger brother, General Charles Churchill, and the guns of Colonel Blood. Apart from the Captain-General and a handful of his staff, no one had any idea where the long march, through the low-lying well-populated country was taking them. The guttural tongues which they heard and the quaint-looking houses that dotted the route convinced Marlborough's men that they were heading for somewhere out of the ordinary. There were some good wines to be had, too, while little cone-shaped hills, crowned here and there with ancient fortresses, provided a fairy-tale picture; and with the local population gay and friendly "Corporal Jack's" army had reason to be in high spirits. Stolid Dutchmen, bewhiskered Prussians, Danes, Hanoverians and scarlet-coated English, they were well satisfied, one and all, that "the Corporal" knew what he was about. They knew too that his first concern was for their welfare, which explains why this astounding march into the heart of a continent was more like a pleasant country stroll on a summer's day. Everything had been thought of for the men's comfort. Marlborough saw to it that they not only suffered as little as possible, but actually gained enjoyment from the adventure.

On the approach to a river, hastily constructed, but none the less reliable, bridges beckoned them across. The daily mileage was covered in the cool of the morning so that by midday, when the next staging camp was reached, the men were still fresh and, with the sun high in the sky, able to appreciate the comforts which their sympathetic and painstaking commander had seen to. Proper meals were a routine feature of the march, even fresh footwear was issued to the needy. The whole operation constituted a masterpiece of detailed planning, inspired by a genius, and moreover, one, who was, unlike the Duke of Wellington, loved rather than feared by his soldiers. For Marlborough's soldiers were his comrades whose lives he strove to preserve even more than his own. The men who fought with Marlborough were kindly treated, well equipped, decently clothed, regularly paid and, above all, properly fed. Attention to detail was, to the Captain-General, a rule of life.

As he rode deep into the heart of Germany, the Captain-General's spirits rose with those of his soldiers. Every mile covered took him further away from meddling English politicians and tiresome Dutch deputies. He felt a new man, relaxed, confident, and yearning for a chance to pit his wits against the much trumpeted Marshals of France.

During the course of the march Marlborough at last made contact with the celebrated Eugene, that Savoy Prince in the Austrian Service without country or wife, a man as single-minded as old Dutch William in his resolve to bring low the arrogant king of France. Famous for his victories over the Turks, Eugene was all fire and nervous energy in contrast to the cool, calculating Englishman. Yet these two great soldiers were on the threshold of a triumphant military partnership such as the world had never before seen. It was not simply the armies they led that bound the two together. They developed a personal respect and affection for one another and an uncanny

Eugene, the great warrior prince of the State of Savoy

mutual understanding, besides which no spark of jealousy ever crept between them, and whatever their differences in council, they always acted in complete accord. At this, their first meeting, at the town of Mendelsheim, the Duke was turned fifty-four, still handsome if a little portly, the Prince only forty-one, but with a score of victories to his credit and dedicated to war. What passed between the two is not recorded. We only know that they took to each other from the very start and, after a sumptuous banquet, for once at the Duke's expense, sat up far into the night, drawing upon each other's genius.

42

At the end of June, with the Rhine far behind them, the Duke's men marched into the valley of the graceful Danube. As they penetrated the Black Forest, heavy rains caused a good deal of sickness, but the Duke in his wisdom, had taken care of this, as of all else. Medical facilities were readily available and recovery was quick.

As the Danube itself hove into sight of Marlborough's men a large force under the Elector of Bavaria and Marshal Marsin was reported to be concentrating a few miles up river, awaiting imminent reinforcement by Marshal Tallard's Frenchmen, at present away to the north-west, on the Rhine. Marlborough, with his long march at last completed, had not a moment to lose. Before staging his battle he meant to gain a bridgehead over the Danube. To this end he decided to seize Donauworth, with its fortified hill of the Schellenberg, which not only dominated the Danube, but was the key to the entry into Bavaria. Meantime the Elector of Bavaria had not been idle. He too appreciated the importance of the Schellenberg and poured as many troops as he could into the stronghold to bolster its defences.

For Marlborough it was a race against time. He must, with his superior force, capture the heights before enemy reinforcements arrived to obstruct him. At first light on June 2, 1704, the Duke could be spotted trotting with his advance guard a ong the muddy road running parallel to the north bank of the Danube in the direction of Donauworth. By breakfast time he could be picked out, a prominent figure in tricorne hat, scarlet coated and with black-topped boots, a good way ahead

Part of the assault on the Schellenberg

of the main body, peering purposefully through his telescope at the newly constructed Bavarian defences. The future of Europe depended, fate decreed, on this high-domed hill dominating the eastern walls of the town, crowned by the fortress of Gustavas, named after the famous Swedish king who had once captured the hill.

Suddenly there burst upon the quiet scene a messenger bringing news that Marshal Tallard had decamped from the Rhine and was marching through the Black Forest in order to link up with Marsin and the Elector on the Danube. The Duke had not a minute to lose.

For tactical reasons the attack on the Schellenberg had to be delivered up the steepest part of the slope, an unpleasant decision for Marlborough with his hatred of large-scale blood-letting. At six o'clock in the evening a force of sixteen battalions, of which five only were British, the remainder mostly Dutch, accompanied by cavalry, advanced uphill in perfect order to within a few yards of the Bavarian defences. Suddenly they were subjected to a merciless fire which decimated their ranks and forced them to withdraw to the bottom again. Bavarian bayonets and grapeshot having done their work well, Marlborough's second assault proved equally bloody, and the Duke, though outwardly calm and confident, was seriously concerned at the dreadful tally being taken amongst the senior ranks, including General Goor, who fell at the head of his sturdy Dutchmen.

With the second assault no more successful than the first, the imperturbable commander received the badly shaken survivors. Spurring them on to fresh endeavour the Duke, with the fate of Europe in his hands, mounted a third attack, this time reinforced by Austrian troops under a senior general of the Empire, Prince Lewis of Baden, who appeared in the rear of the defenders. This tipped the balance. The Bavarians with their rear virtually undefended, fled for their lives down the reverse slope of the hill. Many were drowned in the Danube, whilst others who got across, were cut to pieces by the sharp sabres of the Duke's cavalry.

Out of the 12,000 men of the Elector's army, who had sought to hold the Schellenberg, some 9,000 were put out of action, but the Allied casualty rate was alarmingly high, 5,000 in all, the English infantry having lost one man in every three.

By sunset the battle of the Schellenberg was all over. It had been a dour fight which the humane Duke would have avoided if he could. But the way was now clear for entry into the vast open plain of Bavaria, an expanse of corn alternating with dark forest. The Duke had gained his bridgehead over the Danube and, equally important, he was now securely sandwiched between threatened Austria and the converging French armies. It was a vital achievement and a splendid culmination to his staggering march of over 250 miles. Europe was in a fever of excitement, and awaited the next move. In England there was great joy tempered by scornful Tory comments on the heavy loss of life involved in Marlborough's escapade.

The Duke had no sooner stormed the Schellenberg than he settled down under a hot July sun to the occupation of Bavaria,

46

Marlborough's soldiers laid waste to much of Bavaria

ever hopeful that the Elector might, through subtle persuasion, agree to change sides—and he nearly did. Only the news of Tallard's approach, with another 35,000 Frenchmen, deterred the Elector from accepting Marlborough's lavish bribe to come over to the Allies. But the ever resourceful Duke next tried a policy of coercion. He reluctantly set about the devastation of Bavaria, not only in the hope of bringing the Elector's subjects to heel, but in order to deny food and succour to the invaders.

With the junction of Tallard's and Marsin's and the Elector's rapidly approaching forces, Marlborough meant it only too well when he wrote: "I very much depend on the vigilance of Prince Eugene." The Duke's headaches hit him hard, as he awaited, with deepening anxiety, the arrival of the Prince, who rode with his Austrians over a parallel route from the Rhine. Nor were Marlborough's worries eased by the thought that Marshal Villeroi, now on the Rhine, was liable at any time to detach further French forces to reinforce the large mass on the Danube. Armies were converging on a vast scale. The prelude to the Schellenberg was repeating itself and time was running out. There must be no delay in bringing Tallard and Marsin to battle. After all, that was the sole reason why Marlborough had come all this way. Besides, the Hungarian rebels were ravaging Austria within thirty miles of the capital.

At last, Eugene rode into the Duke's headquarters and the two captains discussed their plans. As a first step, Louis, Margrave of Baden, had to be side-tracked. This prickly and jealous potentate, who had played a gallant though subordinate part at the Schellenberg, could not forgive Marlborough his victory, there having been an arrangement, typical of Marlborough's tact, whereby Marlborough and Prince Louis commanded the Allied army on alternate days. On July 2 when the battle for Schellenberg was fought, it had happened to be the turn of Marlborough, and just as well, for Prince Louis, brave though he was, possessed not one particle of the Englishman's genius for military strategy, though one would not have known it, such was his high opinion of himself.

With jealous memories of the Schellenberg still eating into

Marshal Tallard, one of France's leading generals

his soul, Prince Louis was utterly opposed to a battle. But Marlborough and Eugene fooled him by persuading him to march off with 15,000 men to besiege a fortress, further east, along the Danube. That was a formidable force he was taking with him, but it was a price that the two generals were willing to pay for his absence. Marlborough, a man well versed in trickery, had succeeded once again, and this time in a really good cause, so with revived spirits he crossed to the north of the Danube to meet up once more with Eugene.

Not far to the west was gathered the combined French and Bavarian force, in strength roughly equal to the allies, but with more guns at their disposal. Cautiously the enemy had at

D

first moved eastwards, intent solely on overpowering by sheer numbers, the 18,000 under Prince Eugene. But with Marlborough on the scene the whole complexion had changed. A battle was unthinkable.

After a heated discussion the French Marshals, Tallard and Marsin and the Elector, none of whom appeared to be in overall authority, decided to pitch camp over an expanse of stubble field stretching four miles in breadth between the tiny village of Blenheim, touching the north bank of the Danube, and the thickly wooded hills behind Lutzingen. While the French whitecoats followed the leisurely routine of erecting tents and preparing field kitchens, five miles eastward, a couple of resolute generals leant over a church parapet and, searching through their telescopes, discovered tents going up on rising ground on the far side of a marshy stream. The Duke and the Prince looked at each other with grim satisfaction. The great march had not been in vain. The enemy, unknown to themselves, were making full-scale battle possible through the hurried deployment of their armies. So the immaculate Englishman and the untidy, stooping Savoyard Prince, as opposite in appearance as they were united in purpose, made their plan and, without ceremony, rode their different ways to tell their soldiers all about it.

THE BATTLE OF BLENHEIM

FROM the leisurely movements which the Allied leaders detected through their telescopes the enemy had been well and truly deceived. The armies of France were not attuned to battle. So few had been fought in this two-year old war and there seemed no reason why there should be any sudden change of tactics. There were further indications to support this view. English 'prisoners' cunningly 'planted' by Marlborough before nightfall assured their French interrogators that the Allies were retreating, which merely confirmed what the French commander had thought. Those redcoats, whom the French could vaguely pick out on the horizon, must be covering the retreat northward of Marlborough's army. The possibility that they might have the impudence to attack never occurred to Louis XIV's grand army, as it stood behind the marshes in a line protected on its right flank by the Danube and away on its left, by the pine forests above Lutzingen.

The night before Blenheim was partly spent by the Duke in prayer. Then, at the approach of dawn, he visited Prince Eugene whom he found immersed in correspondence. Both Allied generals, it should be remembered, besides making ready for battle, had still to deal with the endless military problems besetting the kingdoms, whose servants they were. When not thinking about the French, Eugene had to consider

Three allied soldiers: officer of the Swiss Regiment, Austrian officer of heavy cavalry and a British grenadier

ways and means of coping with Hungarian rebellion just as Marlborough had from time to time to devote his attention to the Mediterranean, to Spain, Italy and elsewhere.

As the regiments and squadrons moved off, at first light, to their battle stations, with the Duke's six-horse carriage following, the two commanders were astride their horses, putting the finishing touches to their plan before taking leave of each other.

At the approach of daylight on August 13, the mist cleared, giving way to bright sunshine which lit up the colourful scene set on the north bend of the great river. The variety of uniforms, red, white, blue, many partly obscured by shining breastplates, lent the Danube plain an air of pageantry. There was also a sense of urgency about. The pounding of horses' hooves speeding north to join Eugene, the rattle of cannon in the centre, the shouting of orders as the soldiers, in parade ground fashion, went through their drill to the beat of drums. Everywhere was movement and high tension.

As the Captain-General sat on his horse in a central position, facing the white-coated flower of France, he took stock of the situation before him. To his left flowed the Danube, its glistening surface obscured for a moment by the buildings dotted about in Blenheim village, only to re-appear beyond the spires and gabled roofs to continue its course towards the horizon. To the Duke's immediate front stretched an expanse of hedgeless cornfield for a mile or so down to the Nebel stream, which, leaving the Danube at right angles, meandered past the front of Blenheim, then northwards for three miles up to Lutzingen.

But, looking through his telescope, Marlborough was mainly intent on the picture which presented itself on the far side of the stream to his front. The enemy were encamped on marshy ground behind Blenheim on Marlborough's left as far as the pine covered hills above Lutzingen.

But what of Marshal Tallard, as he rode his horse under the early morning sun? The hectic movements on the far side of

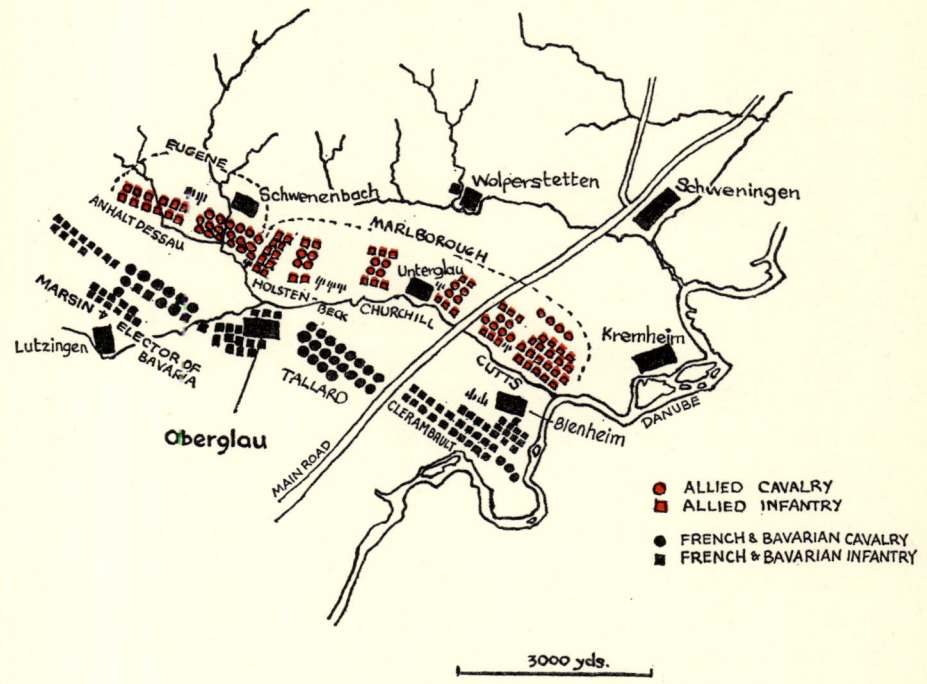

EUGENE
Schwenenbach
Wolperstetten
Schweningen
ANHALT DESSAU
MARLBOROUGH
Unterglau
HOLSTEN-Beck CHURCHILL
Kremheim
MARSIN ELECTOR OF BAVARIA
Lutzingen
TALLARD
CUTTS
Oberglau
Blenheim
DANUBE
CLERAMBAULT
MAIN ROAD

● ALLIED CAVALRY
■ ALLIED INFANTRY

● FRENCH & BAVARIAN CAVALRY
■ FRENCH & BAVARIAN INFANTRY

3000 yds.

The line-up of forces before the Battle of Blenheim

the stream confirmed the reports of the English 'prisoners'. The thin line of redcoats was no less than a covering operation for the general retreat of the Allied army. "It looks as though they will march this day", he wrote to his king, little realizing in which direction. But he was soon undeceived. By breakfast time, not fewer, but more and more soldiers appeared through his telescope as squadron after squadron of horsemen and an unending line of infantry were boldly advancing towards the stream. The French suddenly realized that far from witnessing the retreat of the enemy, they were about to be attacked.

All the while Marlborough, from his central position, telescope in hand, observed the white-coated infantry of France all in a flurry racing to battle stations, senior officers and aides-de-camp galloping up and down in a frantic effort to post their men to the best advantage and in time to meet the onslaught which was being prepared for them. Many, Marlborough carefully noted, made straight for Blenheim village.

Awakened from their slumbers by a rough nudge in the ribs from warrant officers, reinforced by the warning thud of cannon, the French soldiers' spirits were shaken and confidence in their leaders evaporated quickly. They were confronted with the unexpected, the Duke and the Prince having from the very start taken a firm grip on the plan of campaign, in contrast to the all-pervading hesitancy which characterized the divided leadership in the Franco-Bavarian camp.

The opposing armies numbered each about 52,000 and of Marlborough's army about 9,000 were British, the rest a mixture of Dutch, Hessians, Austrians, Hanoverians and Danes. But whatever their differences in nationality the Allied soldiers were single-minded in their resolve to bring low the mighty King of France who had been troubling Europe for so long.

The cool Englishman in command, immaculate as ever, in red tunic, top boots and blue garter sash, his tricorne hat resting lightly on his powdered periwig, exuded confidence as he sat astride his horse, working out odds and contemplating the significance of every hedge, ditch, hut, cornstook, hill and decline.

The plan that both allied commanders had agreed upon the previous night, was, like all the best plans, a simple one—to contain the strongly entrenched enemy flanks while they delivered a belly-punch in the centre.

Tallard, completely taken by surprise by the deployment of Marlborough's entire army on the other side of the stream, acted in understandable haste, and most unwisely. No commander worth his salt should have locked up twenty-seven battalions in tiny Blenheim village, leaving a mere nine to support, as best they could, his massed cavalry in the centre. Marlborough's dispositions covering the southern flank and the centre were the result of forethought. Tallard's smacked of improvisation. His larger Franco-Bavarian army was extended along a two mile front, leaving Marshal Marsin and the Elector's 25,000 Bavarians responsible for the northern flank in front of and to the right of Lutzingen, and stretching northwards as far as the hills.

Marlborough reviewing his troops before the battle

From nine o'clock to midday the two armies glared at one another from opposite sides of the stream. But all was not motionless. Marlborough set some of his soldiers laying planks and faggots across the marshes of the Nebel. Prayers were said in different languages, and Marlborough, a conscientious member of the Church of England, knelt down too and prayed, having already received the sacrament the evening before. The religious observance over, the bands struck up, drum and

The British brigade, led by Brigadier Rowe, stormed the palisade

fife, cymbal and flute, melling with the repetitive booming of cannon. At last the great Duke, a distinguished figure on his white horse, rode past his men as though at a review in Hyde Park. Then, suddenly, the unexpected brought everyone up with a jerk. By now the answering French cannonade had intensified and a shot landed within a few feet of the Duke. There was consternation on every face until, within seconds, which seemed like hours, he flicked off the dust and resumed his stately trot.

After the inspection he munched his picnic lunch in the corn, to all appearances without a care. But the gentle smile which illuminates his handsome features is deceptive, especially to his staff gathered around him. Actually, he is in a fever of anxiety for news of Eugene. Battle proper could not be joined until the Prince was in position away to the North before Lutzingen. But in the late morning he was still feeling his way over rough and broken country in his northward prod. Nor was his progress assisted by a vicious bombardment which was taking an alarming toll of his ranks. In truth, the increasing French cannonade was causing alarming casualties over a wide field and making Marlborough's men more and more impatient to settle matters.

At last Marlborough's iron control was rewarded. A messenger galloped in from the north to announce that Eugene was in position. "His Highness", the messenger tells the Duke, "will give the signal for attack at 12.30." The Duke quietly stood up, and, always one to remember his manners, courteously gave the order, "Gentlemen, to your posts." Now the

60

Allied troops serving their gun

drums beat loud, swords and bayonets flashed under the
midday sun, proud standards fluttered gently in the wind as
the men of Marlborough's army advanced towards the marshy
edges of the Nebel, the fate of Europe in their knapsacks.

On the Allied left sixteen infantry battalions made for
Blenheim itself, where Tallard in his haste had foolishly
cooped up most of the French infantry battalions and twelve
squadrons of dragoons, a waste of fine fighting material which

could have been put to far better use in strengthening his centre. Marlborough was determined to stop them from getting out of the village while he plunged at the enemy's weak spot in the centre. He knew that, like the Schellenberg it would be a gory business and one odious to a man of his humanity. But the enemy had to be contained and an assault had to be put in. Its commander, the intrepid Lord Cutts, known as the Salamanda, was a veteran leader of storming parties with the same indifference to danger as the two Allied commanders. The operation went according to plan. The British brigade followed Brigadier Rowe's order to conserve ammunition by withholding fire until he himself reached the enemy stockade and struck his sword on the palisade. Through a hail of bullets the redcoats advanced unflinchingly at a steady pace, their muskets at the ready, but without a bullet escaping. Despite great gaps in their ranks the advance continued.

At last, the Brigadier, true to his word, touched the palisade and paid the price of bravery by dying a hero's death. The redcoats returned fire, but the French concentration was so intense that the decimated ranks of the leading companies recoiled in disorder, to be replaced by fresh troops, who repeated the process all over again. They too halted before the massive barrier of upturned carts, tables, doors and hedges which comprised the enemy defences. Then, they fired their muskets and withdrew, leaving the dead and dying strewn all over the ground. But no matter what the cost Cutt's men were manfully distracting 12,000 French soldiers so that Marlborough, always in the right place at the right time, could gain his victory over the enemy's weakest spot, in the centre. Their unpleasant task they performed with dogged devotion.

The piercing of the French centre was an operation so vital to the outcome of the battle, as well as to the fortunes of Europe, that the Duke, in his wisdom, gave it his personal attention. First across the Nebel's roughly prepared bridges were General Charles Churchill's foot soldiers, regiment upon regiment of them, marching in disciplined formation, indifferent to the musketry and grapeshot which created such havoc in their ranks. Once on the other side, and with no enemy posted on the edge of the marshy ground to push them

The Allied cavalry charge at Blenheim

back, they fanned out to protect the crossing of the Duke's cavalry.

Now it was Marshal Tallard's turn to make a positive contribution. So far he had done little but make hasty and ill-considered dispositions and gallop uninvited to the left flank where Marsin and the Bavarian Elector had their defences well in hand. With Marlborough now across the Nebel, Tallard, better late than never, launched his horse, thereby setting the scene for the greatest cavalry battle of the century, which, as the afternoon progressed, went gradually more and more Marlborough's way—and for a very good reason. The Allied infantry was so drawn up as to allow the cavalry to withdraw behind it for shelter. Tallard's nine infantry battalions, a hopelessly inadequate force of young recruits for the most part, were simply mown down by the Allied infantry and pulverized by the guns, which Marlborough had carefully sighted to fire at point blank range.

While Marlborough's central cavalry battle was in full swing Prince Eugene, up in the north, had not been idle. His task of containing the French left was, like Cutt's to the south, no easy one. Marsin, in many ways a more skilful general than Tallard, had his men drawn up in sound defensive positions in front of Lutzingen. Eugene's containing action against the Franco-Bavarian force opposed to him, was drawn out and expensive in lives, but equally with Cutt's containing action further south, essential for victory. At a critical moment when Marlborough's forces were in serious danger of being cut off from Eugene further north, through a sudden sortie by

Prince Eugene shoots two of his own men who were attempting to take refuge from the battle

E

Tallard's Irish brigade, Eugene, ever the selfless friend, and indeed hard-pressed himself, restored the balance by sending the Duke a whole brigade of his own.

At five o'clock a curious lull descended on the battlefield. The Allied position was not all it might be and time was getting on. In his isolated position on the Danube, 250 miles from whence he had set out, the Duke could not afford a drawn battle, least of all a defeat. He had to win soon, but at five o'clock that summer's evening the situation was far from rosy. The Blenheim action had proved more costly than had been hoped. The central cavalry battle was still undecided, while on the Allied right, before Lutzingen, Eugene's inspiring leadership had failed so far to shake the stronger forces of the Bavarian Elector and Marshal Marsin. Despite constant pleas to renew their efforts his men were exhausted and the Prince, all fire and brimstone in the heat of the battle, actually shot two fugitives with his own pistol—a hot-headed action in marked contrast to the Duke's polite rebuke to a cavalry general he spotted riding away from the field. "M—", said the Duke in that soft voice of his, "You are under a mistake; the enemy lies that way; you have nothing to do, but to face him and the day is your own."

At one stage the Prince was so disgusted by his own Imperial cavalry for failing to come up to his own high standards of bravery, that he shouted he would prefer to die with Prussian and Danish infantry than fight with cowards.

But, whatever others felt, the Duke himself was confident of victory. Here in the centre was the crux and here more and

66

The French cavalry were driven to the Danube, where many disappeared over the high banks

more men were pouring across the stream and fanning out the other side to support the cavalry. Marlborough was building up a gradual preponderance which must in the end turn the tables, especially with 12,000 men marooned in Blenheim, unable to lend any help. In the early stages the Duke had fewer troops, largely through the toll taken by the initial French cannonade, but being the master gambler he was, he knew that he was now narrowing the odds with a vengeance.

With the sun still high in the sky the Duke, who had risked battle against all advice, knew that his tactics had paid off and his hour had struck. By six o'clock he had built up in the centre a majority of three to one, and he held an additional ace in his hand. Tallard's young French soldiers, their white coats now bloodstained and damp with the sweat of battle, were completely demoralized. Impassive and cool, "Corporal Jack" drew his sword and set the bugles blowing. With one accord the cavalry squadrons, beginning with a trot, broke into a gallop, sweeping all before them. The French horsemen, together with what remained of the nine infantry battalions, were swept towards the Danube, where thousands of men and horses disappeared for ever over the high banks.

Marshal Tallard, already miserable at the loss of his son, made for Blenheim, resolved to extricate his twenty-seven battalions or die in the attempt. As it happened, he never reached the village, for on the way he fell into the hands of German cavalry, who could see from the star emblazoned on his richly embroidered coat that he was no ordinary officer. Appreciating, for once, the true situation, the French Marshal consented, with resignation, to being escorted to the Duke.

The English commander remained meanwhile astride his horse beyond the Nebel, surrounded by the wounded and the dying, a hideous aspect of battle which he loathed with all his heart. Many of his detractors dismissed Marlborough as a cold creature, but those close to him in war, knew better. They saw in him only a deep humanity.

To the north, Eugene's Germans had had their fill of attack, retreat and counter-attack and were in no state to give chase. Marsin and the Elector thus escaped in the gathering dusk westwards in good order. Yet the Prince had done his work nobly. By containing a much larger force before Lutzingen he had allowed his friend to triumph further south. His contribution to the great victory was second only to the Duke's.

With the approach of darkness, Cutts in the south had been reinforced from Marlborough's victorious centre. Blenheim came under siege, the dreaded river Danube providing the only means of escape, but an unpleasant prospect with Marlborough's horsemen hovering on its banks.

When the time came, Marlborough, with exquisite courtesy, received the captured French Marshal, and put his coach at his disposal. Only when Tallard, aware of the destruction of his forces in Blenheim, offered to order his men to cease fire, did the Duke speak sharply. "Inform M. Tallard," he said, "that in the position he now is, he has no command."

It was at this winding up stage of the battle that the Duke wrote his famous letter to Sarah, the original of which is now on view at Blenheim Palace. Calling for a stump of pencil he wrote on the back of a tavern bill, "I have not time to say more, but to beg you will give my duty to the Queen and let her know her army has had a glorious victory. Monsieur Tallard and two other generals are in my coach and I am following the rest. . . ."

Before night closed in five separate attempts were made to capture Blenheim, but none proved successful and all expensive. Fortunately, the bloodshed came to an end far quicker than might have been expected when the Earl of Orkney called the bluff of a French officer, who agreed to surrender and, more important, managed to persuade his brother officers to do likewise. There followed scenes of bitter dismay in the village as regiment upon regiment stamped on its colours and, in a fury, set them alight. By the time Marlborough came over to wind up the battle the defenders of Blenheim were prisoners to a man. The losses in the village were high, but at least 9,000 unwounded soldiers, which included the most illustrious regiments in all France, laid down their arms.

On that bright summer's day two-thirds of the French army were destroyed or captured and the remainder obliged to retreat over the hills. At about 9 p.m. the captured battalions, their own men dazed, filed out of the village to their bivouacs in the open ground. There they were guarded by tired, but happy men of the British infantry, their bayonets fixed, their duty almost done. Of Blenheim, Orkney later wrote, "It is perhaps the greatest and completest victory that has been gained these many ages."

Within eight days the news burst upon England. Colonel Park, with the Duke's crumpled tavern bill in his knapsack, rode for all he was worth across Europe before crossing the Channel and resuming his ride to London. There he tarried only long enough to tell Sarah how her husband had saved Europe, before setting out for the last lap of his journey, to Windsor Castle. When Queen Anne heard of "Mr Freeman's victory" she was so overjoyed that the £500 it was customary to give the bearer of victorious news was doubled. Colonel Park received £1,000 and the Queen's portrait in miniature.

In London itself the cannon in the Tower boomed out the joy of the whole people. The church bells chimed and coffee

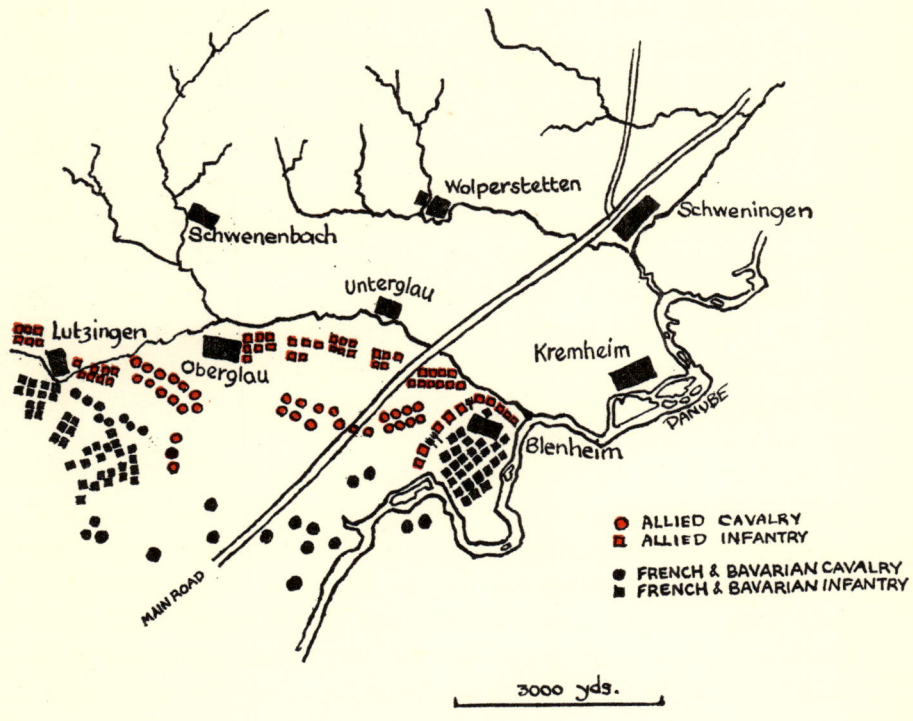

Schwenenbach

Wolperstetten

Schweningen

Unterglau

Lutzingen

Oberglau

Kremheim

Blenheim

DANUBE

MAIN ROAD

● ALLIED CAVALRY
■ ALLIED INFANTRY

● FRENCH & BAVARIAN CAVALRY
■ FRENCH & BAVARIAN INFANTRY

3000 yds.

Towards the close of the battle the French middle was broken and many were
cornered by the river Danube

Queen Anne receives Marlborough's
message, proclaiming his great victory

houses and ale houses were packed to overflowing with folk of all kinds, men and women, young and old, high and low, all with but one aim—to drink the Queen's health and that of the great soldier whose wonderful victory had brought lustre to her throne.

On the night of the battle "Corporal Jack", always the soldier's soldier, laid his weary body upon the ground and speedily fell into a deep sleep under the stars. Like certain other great captains, Marlborough's physical needs were small. Moreover, he required neither panoply nor pomp to bolster his ego. His deeds were plain for all to see.

AFTER THE BATTLE

BLENHEIM made of Marlborough an international figure overnight. At the beginning of the campaign he was hardly known outside his own country, but when the news of his victory burst upon a startled Europe, his name was at once a household word, more celebrated even than that of his great friend, the Prince of Savoy.

The battle had cost the Allies about 5,000 killed and 8,000 wounded, mostly from amongst Eugene's force. The French army, that magnificent body of men, which till this moment had known nothing of defeat, was almost entirely destroyed. Of the 60,000 men who on that misty morning had stood to arms close by the Danube, only 20,000, a mere third, were ever to fight again. That day 12,000 French soldiers were killed, 14,000 made prisoner, including the commanding general and over 1,000 officers of distinction, while the Allies helped themselves to all the cannon, colours and standards they could lay their hands on, not to speak of tents untold and other appurtenances of war.

City after city, notably Ulm, Landau and Trèves, surrendered to the Allies before the year 1704 was out. Bavaria submitted to the Austrian Emperor, and on the far side of Vienna, the Hungarian rebels laid down their arms. Austria was saved and the military ascendancy of the Allies completely established. From that moment Vienna was safe and the Sun

King could never again take the offensive in Germany. His demoralized army retreated right back to France. Blenheim might put a stop, once and for all, to Louis' vision of world conquest. There had been no English victory like it for three hundred years, not since Henry V scattered the nobility of France at Agincourt.

Marlborough was inevitably the hero of the hour. England acclaimed him: her partners in the Grand Alliance even more. But in the aftermath of battle there was to be no peace for him. He was something else besides the victor of Blenheim. As presiding genius of the Grand Alliance he carried a massive burden, involving uncomfortable coach rides the length and breadth of the Continent. He had only to show himself in one of Europe's capitals, for a tumultuous crowd to press in on him and shout their plaudits to the roof-tops.

The grateful Emperor, to save whose throne the Duke had staked his whole career, offered to make the Duke a sovereign Prince of the Holy Roman Empire, and, although he afterwards repented of his generosity, the Duke held him to his word and eventually received the principality of Mindelheim in Swabia. Blenheim made of Marlborough a kind of hero even to his enemies. "Marlborough s'en va t'en guerre" was a song now on every French soldier's lips while in England the leading whig poet, Joseph Addison, had this to say of the great soldier:

> "Twas then great Marlborough's mighty soul was proved
> That in the shock of charging hosts unmoved,
> Amidst confusion, horror and despair,

In peaceful thought the field of death surveyed,
To fainting squadrons sent the timely aid,
Inspired repulsed battalions to engage,
And taught the doubtful battle where to rage.
So when an angel by divine command,
With rising tempests shakes a guilty land,
Such as of late o'er Britannia passed,
Calm and serene he drives the furious blast;
And, pleased th'Almighty's order to perform,
Rides in the whirlwind and directs the storm."

With his diplomatic travels completed, Marlborough arrived in London in December, 1704, accompanied by Marshal Tallard and sixteen French generals, together with an impressive collection of colours and standards captured at

The victory march through the streets of London, with many of the captured French and Bavarian colours

Blenheim. They were paraded through the London streets before coming to rest in the Tower, where not so very long ago the Duke himself had been housed, though it seemed hardly believable with all the compliments and hospitality now being showered upon him. Much as the Duke enjoyed his new-found popularity he enjoyed even more the £5,000 a year, voted him by Parliament, and, more still, the precious gift with which a grateful Queen chose to present him.

To commemorate his great victory he was given the royal manor park of Woodstock, near Oxford, where the famous architect, Sir John Vanburgh, was commissioned to build a palace. In the years ahead it was to absorb much of Marlborough's time, but it remained uncompleted at his death. It was left to Sarah, the eccentric widow who outlived the Duke by many years, to see to the finishing touches. Blenheim Palace in the end cost the nation all of £240,000, which in terms of 18th century currency, represents a fantastic figure. It remains to this day about the most imposing building in England, a truly noble monument to the achievement of a great man, but a home, never. Even the trees are planted according to the formation of Marlborough's horse and foot at Blenheim.

This great battle, then, was fully celebrated in the honours bestowed upon the Duke through verse, through bricks and mortar and through something closer to his heart—money. But it signified only the start of the high noon of his career. Within two years he fought Ramillies (1706), a set-piece battle which had Villeroi completely flawed right from the booming of the preliminary cannonade until the stricken French Marshal found himself being propelled into headlong flight after losing half his army. Blenheim, the Duke's enemies at home attributed to luck, reinforced by the presence of Eugene. After Ramillies, from which the Prince of Savoy was conspicuously absent, they kept quiet. What, after all, could they say in criticism of a man whose second victory led both to the conquest of Belgium and to the complete moral collapse of the French army? As an able French Marshal told his king at the time, "Everyone is ready to take off his hat at the mere mention of Marlborough." Brussels opened its gates for the hero to pass through.

The victory of Ramillies, often regarded as the Duke's masterpiece, coincided with the year of Prince Eugene's victories in Northern Italy. After a lengthy march reminiscent of Marlborough's before Blenheim, the Prince relieved Turin, the capital of Lombardy in a superb action against heavy odds which led to the eventual flight of the French from Northern Italy. This was followed by further successes, confined for a change to the diplomatic field; for the Duke, it should be remembered, was no less adept at diplomacy than he was at fighting. His winning ways, his immense tact, inexhaustible patience and subtle brain, stood him in good stead when dealing with kings and potentates. One such was the sabre-rattling young Charles XII of Sweden, whom Marlborough managed to persuade to leave the West alone and instead concentrate all his energies against Russia.

No sooner was that mission complete than early in July,

1708, Marshal Vendôme was reported to have captured two of Belgium's chief towns, Bruges and Ghent, and to be threatening a third, Oudenarde. Quick as lightning, Marlborough moved his army into position between the French and this old fortress town, and in a battle, whose fortunes fluctuated from minute to minute, dealt another hammer blow to the French army, which only nightfall rendered incomplete. Eugene again brought his great martial talents to bear on the proceedings, but, as always, he took his orders from the Duke. Later that year Marlborough turned his talents to siege warfare by investing Lille. It was a tough proposition, and only after many weeks, and at a huge loss, did this, the strongest fortress of France, finally yield. During his eleven campaigns the Duke laid siege to many other fortresses. In fact, as already mentioned, he took more than any other English general in history.

There were other battles before the war was over, notably the Battle of Malplaquet (1709), in which Marlborough and Eugene suffered heavy losses. Then within a year of Malplaquet, Marlborough, whose mastery of warfare had raised his country's prestige to a height hitherto unknown, was dismissed from all his offices, civil and military, and life made so unbearable that he and Sarah were forced into exile. How could this come about after what he had achieved? The answer is simple. Sarah, so long the Queen's bosom friend and confidante, grew so overbearing that Queen Anne tired of her and when another lady-in-waiting insinuated her way into the royal favours, decided to have done with her friendship.

78

After one last stormy scene the hysterical Duchess left the Palace of Westminster for the last time, and from that moment, despite the glories he continued to gain on the Continent, the Duke's fortunes began to deteriorate.

Stripped at last of royal support and with Godolphin, his loyal old friend, dead, Marlborough quickly became a target for jealous politicians, who accused him of harbouring the ambitions of a Cromwell. In the popular press which was now beginning to blossom, there were plenty of hacks only too willing to pour vitriol on the Duke's good name if it would earn them a penny or two from their political paymasters.

While Marlborough was out of the country the politicians made peace at Utrecht. But they saw to it that the glories of Blenheim and Ramillies were dimmed. Since Marlborough's dismissal the fortunes of France revived to the extent that England's waned under the Tories who now directed a Continental war, which they had always opposed, in a half-hearted manner, till it finally fizzled out altogether. By the Treaty of Utrecht (1713) England gained colonies from Spain and France while Philip was allowed to keep Spain provided he made no attempt at any time to join his Crown to that of France. As for France herself, though she could no longer dominate Europe, she retained most of the land which she had so greedily acquired during a half-century of aggression. On the whole the Treaty of Utrecht ensured that the balance of power, before Blenheim tipped so heavily in France's favour, was now safely restored and the great king's grandiose schemes for the subjugation of a continent lay in ashes.

George I's accession in 1714 brought about a revival in the Marlborough fortunes. The Duke and Duchess crossed the Channel once more to be greeted by the new king in terms of genuine affection. All the Duke's high offices were restored and the great man, a semi-invalid now, was left in peace, to spend the evening of his life at the great palace of Blenheim with his Duchess who loved him as much as on the day they married. It was not until June 16, 1722, that death came at the age of 72 to one of England's greatest generals—the man whose skill and daring saved a continent from complete subjugation midst those distant cornfields beside the Danube.